KT-367-252

# DOG
## BODY LANGUAGE
# PHRASEBOOK

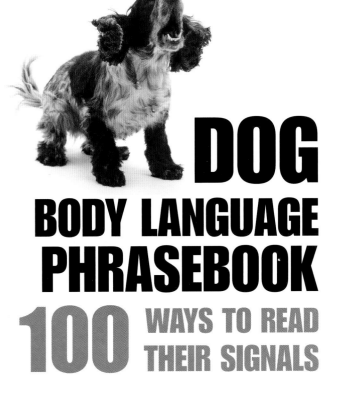

# DOG
# BODY LANGUAGE
# PHRASEBOOK
# 100 WAYS TO READ THEIR SIGNALS

## Trevor Warner

SALAMANDER

Published in 2007 by Salamander Books
10 Southcombe Street, London, W10 0RA

An imprint of Anova Books Company Ltd.
Copyright © Salamander Books 2007

All rights reserved. No part of this publication may be reproduced, stored in a retrieval system, or transmitted in any form or by any means, electronic, mechanical, photocopying, recording or otherwise, without prior written permission of the copyright owner.

10 9 8 7 6 5 4 3 2 1

ISBN: 978-1-84065-567-4

Printed in China

# Contents

# Introduction

The dog is man's best friend. Ever since it evolved from its wolflike ancestor and was domesticated by early humans, the dog has been a useful addition to the family. In early times it was put to use as a guard dog, warning of attack or attempts to steal precious livestock. Its role as guard was later extended, and dogs were used as hunting aids, to help in the herding and driving of animals, and to control pests.

In the third millennium, dogs perform a huge range of functions for their masters, acting as hearing dogs, guide dogs, and police dogs for sniffing out drugs and explosives, and yet they still perform the one role for which they were recruited from the wild—that of faithful guard.

Today the role of guard is an incidental one; above all else, the dog is there as a pet: a loving, faithful, and trusting companion ready with its unconditional love and tail-wagging enthusiasm.

So what makes it behave the way it does? Why are dogs so willing to take instruction and obey, whereas cats are independent and seem to have their own willful agenda? To understand dog behavior, one really needs to look at where the dog came from: its wolf ancestors. The wolf evolved into the wild dog and then became domesticated. A dog, in effect, is a wolf in your backyard. Almost all of its behavioral traits are shared by wolves. A pack of African wild dogs deploys itself in exactly the same way as a wolf pack. They work together and in a hierarchy, with a leader assisted by dominant pack members who, in turn, dominate other pack members.

The domestic dog is the same, except instead of a wolf pack it has a family and, providing all is well, it accepts its role as the lowest-status member of the family pack. The reason a dog craves company so much is genetic; it is programmed to be with other dogs. And if not dogs, then humans. That is part of the reason why a dog will not desert its dying master—it won't leave the leader of the pack.

From the earliest domesticated dogs, selective breeding has produced a vast range of dog varieties, from the towering Irish wolfhound to the tiny Yorkshire terrier. It's amazing to think that in medieval Europe there were only about twenty recognizable breeds. Today there are over 700, and as dog breeders strive to produce thoroughbred dogs with a particular trait, that number will increase. All breeds have behavioral characteristics that can be traced back to the wolf, and this book will help explain the links.

The single most important factor behind a dog's interaction with other dogs and members of its pack is status—who is top dog? The bid to become top dog starts in puppyhood with all the rough-and-tumble games: the soft bites, the muzzle bumping, and the play-mounting. What starts as fun and games between playmates takes on a more serious slant as they reach adulthood. Quite often, owners see these interactions between adult dogs and dismiss it as "just play"; however, dogs regard it differently. They see the "little victories" over the other pack members as an enhancement of their status; that is why they will race to be first through the gate, take the favorite bone and monopolize it, and hang their necks over their siblings.

It may look petty to humans, but not to dogs. Trouble arrives when dogs start playing petty games with their owners: refusing to let go of toys, insisting on being let into rooms, or sleeping on their owners' bed. On their own, these actions seem pretty harmless, but they are all being logged on the dog's private scorecard. In these situations, the dog starts to think that it is the top dog of the entire house and its behavior degenerates. The assumed top dog, when not given its leader-of-the-pack prominence by its owners, will resort to barks, growls, and violence.

We have recently seen a trend of television programs dedicated to tackling problems just like this. Owners think they are being kind by letting dogs have their own way. However, most of the dog behavioral problems I encounter in my veterinary practice are a result of aggression—and this overkindness by owners is one of the principal causes.

Although this book is intended as an entertaining and not overly scientific look at the way dogs behave, it will give some very important pointers as to how to treat your dog. Dogs work well in a hierarchy, even at the bottom, but they like clear, uncomplicated messages. Most of all, they like consistent messages.

One owner whose dog I treated used exactly the same tone of voice to call his dog as he used to reprimand it. Then he began to wonder why the dog wouldn't come to him when he called. The simple reason was that the dog was fearful of being told off and dealt with the situation

by ignoring his owner. All the owner had to do was alter the calling voice.

I would like to think of this book as a starting point, the first step toward understanding the behavior of your dog. For those who are intrigued by the subject, there are quite a few other books that will give a more comprehensive and scientific basis for what I like to think is common sense. If you have serious or continuing problems with the behavior of your dog, there is no substitute to visiting an animal psychologist or behaviorist. However, be warned. Many pet behaviorists believe that there are few problem dogs—and a lot more problem owners.

**Trevor Warner, 2006**

# "D'you wanna be in my gang?"

Dogs love to be in their own pack—it gives them security as well as companionship and playmates. And if they are in the wild, it helps them get food through hunting together. Packs don't need to be very big for pack tendencies to start showing themselves—it may be as few as two or three dogs. In a house with more than one dog, if a dog shies away from the rest of the pack, it could be that it was brought up alone as a pup and never learned the social techniques it needs for getting along with other dogs.

The pack instinct is just one of the links to a dog's wolf ancestry. In so many ways we can see that a dog's behavior echoes that of wolves.

## BY ROYAL APPOINTMENT

The Afghan hound was once a favorite of royalty and is mentioned in historical texts as far back as 4000 BC. Another royal favorite (in this case, of Queen Elizabeth II) is the Cardigan Welsh corgi (see left), which is thought to be the oldest purebred British dog. The corgi's roots are traced to the Celts in Wales around 1200 BC. (The pup on the far left is still waiting for his ear to develop fully.)

# "I'm all alone!"

Howling is almost always a sign of loneliness or separation. The dog is saying, "Don't leave me, come back!" It feels isolated and the howl is aimed at bringing its owner or even a playmate back. Wolves use the howl to great effect in the wild to bring the pack together. It is the call to assemble the pack. Once a wolf can bring together several members of the pack, the cry will resound across the valley and mountainside to summon all the wolves in the land. With dogs, the howl is almost always solitary, but it serves the same purpose because it is used to bring someone toward them. Bored dogs left alone all day can induce strong reactions in neighbors with their constant howling—phone calls are made, and the owner returns. Howling works!

## !  THE WILDERNESS TELEGRAPH

Wolves use howling both to assemble the pack for hunting and also at the edges of their territory to show other wolf packs where the boundaries lie. When wolves are cast out of a pack, they may use their howl to join a new pack. Given that wolves hunt at night, it's no surprise that the light of a full moon is perfect for hunting . . . and howling.

# "Don't move— I'm in charge."

Three's a pack, two's a hierarchy. Even when there are just two dogs together, one has more status than the other. It will be the one that goes first when the pair have to walk in single file; it will be the one that scores the "little victories" over the other. As we often see in everyday life, it's the tough little individuals who are more driven and come out on top. Pair a Jack Russell terrier with a Great Dane, and it could easily be the Jack Russell who takes command of the duo.

## PUPPY POWER

Puppies try to dominate their littermates by:
- Pouncing on them
- Standing up on their shoulders
- Standing over them with their body held high and at right angles to them—i.e., forming a T shape
- Circling them menacingly
- Using the soft "play" bite in a mock attack
- Body slams
- Muzzle bumping and muzzle biting
- Play-mounting them
- Snarling their teeth
- Staring at them
- Boxing them with their paws

# "I'll stay quiet—you're the boss."

Dogs are happiest when they have a clear social structure. Being at the bottom of the social ladder means it doesn't have to fight to maintain its position—it knows its place! In a family, dogs are at the bottom and will accept that children smaller than themselves are still above them in the hierarchy, just as they will let smaller dogs dominate them in a pack.

Problems arise when a dog thinks it is actually the leader of the household. This can be the result of excessive affection and attention from an owner. The dog starts to believe that because its every wish is granted—walks on demand, food on demand, etc.—that it's now in charge. It will try to dictate who comes into rooms and whether the adults are allowed to sit on furniture.

## DOGGY PADDLE

The massive Newfoundland is a great swimmer and is aided by its webbed feet. However, basset hounds are terrible swimmers. With two-thirds of their weight in the front and such short legs, they can barely keep afloat. If bassets are going to be taken on boats, owners should take life preservers for them.

# "C'mon, this is a great game."

Some humans may be loners, but dogs are not. They need the companionship of others—preferably dogs or humans, but sometimes even cats will do. That's why it's common to see dogs bond with other pets in the household. They love to be with other animals and, just like attention-seeking children, will exhibit extreme behavior to get their "parents" to respond and play games if they're neglected.

# "One down, three to go."

When a bitch gives birth to her litter, she instinctively knows how to cut the umbilical cord and lick the puppies clean. That early smell-recognition process is an important bond. If a birth becomes difficult and a vet needs to deliver the puppies by cesarean section, then a bitch may reject them afterward, especially if they pick up too many unfamiliar smells. Pups emerge at intervals of between five and thirty minutes, giving the bitch just enough time to clean up one before the next arrives.

## ! CRUEL TO BE KIND

When a litter is born in the wild, if a bitch senses there are too many mouths to feed, she will take away the sickliest pups from the litter and leave them to die. If she feels insecure about her location, she will move the nest to a location where she feels safer.

# "Careful does it."

Once the pups are born and start suckling, it is the bitch's job to keep them and the nest clean. She does this by licking all their waste products away. So her reward for having eight puppies hanging off her belly is to go around and clean up their mess afterward. It's a tough job, but someone's got to do it.

## TAKING THE LEAD

Discipline is important for keeping a puppy on the straight and narrow. It's good to take a pup out on a leash to teach it that it has to walk where you want it to. It's also good to start teaching it the basic commands—sit, stay, come, down, and heel—as soon as possible.

# "Chow down!"

Puppies come into the world almost helpless. They are blind and deaf and usually hungry. Unlike cats, who claim one nipple on the mother and stick to it, puppies are much less fussy. For them, suckling time is a case of first come, first served. Depending on how the bitch is lying, there may not be enough nipples showing, so the competitive instinct and the fight for survival begins at an early age.

## ! TOUGH PUPPY LOVE

The golden rule for training pups is that they do something first and it's rewarded afterward. They don't get something for nothing. Unconditional love and affection is not the best training tool! So a good way to start teaching a pup the command to sit is just before it is fed. It does the work, then gets rewarded afterward. Apart from rewarding good behavior, this also emphasizes that you are in control and the puppy is not.

# "Ruff! Wow, was that me who said that?"

Puppies develop quickly, and at three weeks they can wag their tails and emit the occasional tiny bark. It's at this age that they will start taking trips away from the nest to eliminate so the bitch doesn't have to clean up after them. At four weeks, they will start learning the social facts of life and where they fit into the new pack they have joined. They will start to bully and be bullied by other members, and they will also start to copy their parents. So a calm dog with a good attitude toward humans is likely to produce calm puppies.

### SOCIAL SKILLS

"Socialization" among puppies is the process by which they learn how to recognize and interact, first with other dogs, then with humans and maybe also with a few cats. By learning how to interact with all these creatures, the socialized dog develops awareness and communication skills. Socialization helps puppies recognize when they are being threatened and how to respond to the actions of others.

# "Urgh, it's nasty, cold, and wet!"

Puppies are often separated from their littermates at around seven weeks, when the bitch's milk starts to dry up—this is the time when puppies begin to be sold or given away. However, the pup could still be learning important social skills in the eighth and ninth weeks—such as the "soft bite" (or inhibited bite), how to give signals to the rest of the pack, how to play-wrestle, and generally copying their parents and learning what dogs do. Skills not learned in these important early weeks can be lost forever, producing an adult dog that finds it difficult to interact with others. Threshold ages for puppy progress will vary from breed to breed. This inadvertent separation (right) of a puppy from its pack has not been a pleasant experience, but it's all part of the learning process. The puppy has learned that it can't chase butterflies if they fly across the pond.

## ! COLD DOG, HOT DOG

Though dog magazine readers might not be typical of the average dog owner, in a survey over 60 percent of them admitted to owning a sweater, winter coat, or raincoat for their dogs.

# "Ow, that hurt!"

Learning the "soft bite" is a very important part of puppy play. In the early weeks, when they first decide that their littermates are a source of interest, they'll experiment by biting them. This will produce yelps of astonished pain and recriminations that will bring playing to an end and might even need an angry interjection from mom. So they learn instead that a soft, inhibited bite will allow the game to continue without hurting the other pup, who in turn will give soft bites back.

Dogs that have been split up from their littermates and haven't learned the soft bite technique may later bite for real when playing, causing fights and other problems for their owners.

## "I'm on top!"

After five weeks, their eyesight is well developed and puppies will start to gain a curiosity about their world, which they will want to explore (and put in their mouth). Though during the first few weeks of life it was their mother who was the biggest influence on them, now it is their littermates who begin to influence them the most. At this age, they are learning their social skills and how to win little victories in their bid to become top dog—among their littermates, anyway.

# "How long do I have to stay here?"

Though some will have been separated from the pack by now, in weeks seven to ten, puppies are refining their social interactions with their littermates and have a very good idea of their social status within the group. It is important that a puppy has positive experiences with humans from five weeks onward, as these first impressions can last a lifetime. Puppies are now exploring their surroundings even more and are discovering the boundaries of their world. They begin to turn their attention to people now, and so this is a phase where training can begin.

## DON'T GIVE THEM CHOCOLATE

You may have thought it to be a rumor, but it's true; chocolate *can* kill dogs. Chocolate contains theobromine, which in sufficient quantities is toxic to dogs. It takes a fairly large amount of theobromine to cause a toxic reaction, but on average, milk chocolate contains 44 mg of theobromine per ounce; baker's chocolate is far more concentrated, with up to 390 mg per ounce.

# "I could spend hours doing this."

It's a dog fact of life that puppies will go through their chewing phase. This can involve shoes, gloves, magazines, children's toys—whatever the pup can get its teeth into. It's no surprise that gloves and shoes are favorites; they are often smelly and leathery, providing the closest thing to prey that is lurking around the house. Puppies need something to chew on to help their adult teeth start to break through at four months old, and if they don't have a range of leathery chews or rubber toys, they will find one for themselves. Owners who keep their houses neat may have a tendency to tidy up these easily discarded, half-chewed items and so pups, deprived of their chew, will find the nearest substitute.

## IGNORANCE IS BLISS

One of the best ways of treating naughty dogs is to ignore them. For instance, if a dog continually barks when you enter the room, the simplest solution is to immediately leave the room. Being social animals, dogs prefer to be with someone rather than alone. It only needs to be for a few minutes, but the lesson is learned after this is repeated a few times.

# "I need milk— and look, I can still reach!"

Puppies are weaned off milk in a gradual process that starts between three and four weeks. In the wild, the bitch would start to go off hunting and come back and regurgitate half-digested meals; in a domestic environment, she will make the nursing position less and less available to the litter. Even when she does, she may not do it for long and will end a session by getting up and walking away— sometimes with pups still attached!

At five weeks old, milk is no longer available on demand and she might reprimand a puppy that dares to clamor around her. It's tough love. Puppies might gather around and try to feed when she is standing still, but chances are slim and it depends on the mood she's in. Between weeks five and seven, her milk gradually dries up, but owners are quick to provide milk, assuming pups can learn to lap it up rather than suck. The "perpetual puppyhood" starts early.

## PICKING UP THE LITTER

Unlike in the film *101 Dalmatians* where Pongo and Perdita had a litter of fifteen puppies (born pure white as Dalmatian puppies are), the average litter size is around five. Some litters can be as many as twenty, and the largest recorded is twenty-four from a Neapolitan mastiff bitch.

# "Any food in there?"

Signs from puppyhood often carry through into adult life. When a dog tries to lick a human's mouth, it is saying: "You're my mom—you're the boss." In the w77h's mouth to get her to regurgitate a half-digested meal after she has been out hunting. Domestic dogs don't need to go hunting while they're raising a litter, but puppies will still lick their mom's mouth to show that they're hungry.

# "It's mine!"
# "No, it's mine!"
# "I saw it first!"

The competitive pack instinct starts early in pups, and everyone wants to get in on the act. When puppies fetch sticks, they are learning important behaviors. They learn how to interact with the rest of the litter—they can show just who is top dog by getting there first—and they are also sharpening their hunting skills. In the wild, pups would begin hunting at around twelve weeks. Retrieving sticks is a great way to continue that early phase; plus, it's a whole lot easier to catch a thrown stick than a live, darting rabbit. Once the stick-throwing trick is learned in puppyhood, dogs will take it into adulthood and enjoy it even more.

# "I've named three of them so far."

Bitches, even those that have been spayed, sometimes suffer from "phantom pregnancies," where they believe they are about to give birth. They will wander around the house, become unapproachable, and linger in dark, out-of-the-way places. Some of these phantom pregnancies become so advanced that the dogs even produce milk.

Another indication of the phantom pregnancy is when they collect some toys or other items as "token puppies" and create a nest. Animal behaviorists recommend that you administer some tough love and take away the toys (or anything that could be gathered as a token puppy) in the hope that the bitch will snap out of it—which they will after a while.

**!**

### BRAINY DOGS

The dog with the smallest brain-to-body ratio is said to be the Afghan hound. The most intelligent dogs are thought to be poodles, Border collies, and golden retrievers.

# "Milk's great, but why do I have to share?"

A wagging tail isn't always the sign of contentment that it's thought to be. When puppies line up alongside their mother to suckle, the tail wagging can be fast and furious, and the message seems to be: "Hooray, it's feeding time again!" However, the wagging only happens after the pups are several weeks old and is actually more a sign of nervousness than pleasure. This is because, as puppies develop, they get thrown into the commotion of puppy play and the social hierarchies that develop within the litter. When it's time to suckle, they have to dive in together, eager to get milk and at the same time anxious that they suddenly have to nuzzle in close proximity to a pup that seconds earlier might have been trying to bully them. Tail wagging can also be a sign of uncertainty in dogs, and tail wagging by feeding pups shows that conflict of emotion— they want to feed, they're excited that it's feeding time, but they wish they didn't have to get so close to each other.

# "Yo, bro!"

Wagging tails are seen not only on feeding puppies but also when dogs greet their owners, when they greet one another, when they want to play games, during sexual play, and in some aggressive situations. Most humans are used to being greeted by friendly, socialized dogs who are happy to see them, and so the association between tail wagging and "saying hello" is firmly fixed in the human psyche. However, there is also apprehension mixed in with the joy. In a sexual approach, there is the joy of actually finding a member of the opposite sex in heat mixed with the doubt of what is going to happen next. When an owner gets home, there is the joy of being reunited with the pack leader tinged with the uncertainty of whether they'll be ignored in favor of the TV or the other, smaller members of the pack—human children.

## ! THE WAG CLUB

Dogs use tail wagging to waft their scent out into the world. A vigorously wagged tail helps diffuse scent from a dog's anal gland to an appreciative doggy audience.

# "He's been way too long at work."

Being left alone all day, locked up in a house, is bad enough for a dog, but being left alone when a dog can't see what's going on around him is much worse. Though an owner will know he's locked the door and the house is secure, a dog hasn't figured out this "key-in-door" process. From a dog's point of view, a stranger could come through the door at any moment. So if a dog needs to be kept inside, the more space he has to himself the better, and a place to view the passing world is good, too. Most dogs will learn that their house is a safe place where friends are let in and strangers stay on the doorstep, but it's hard for them to figure out the protocol of just who does come inside and why.

## WEIGHTY ISSUES

There are no fat dogs or fat wolves in the wild. Canine obesity is due to lack of exercise and overfeeding. It has been estimated that one of every three domestic dogs is fat, with the problem particularly bad in labradors and spaniels. One theory regarding canine obesity is that dogs are overfed as puppies and a certain level of food intake gets established in their minds. After puppyhood, it's almost impossible to shake off that "need" for more food.

# "I'm so glad you're home."

Though tail wagging is an indication of an excited state, it can be either good excitement or bad excitement. The tail wag that goes from side to side in a wide arc is the characteristic "hello" wag. A wildly wagging tail combined with an eagerness to jump up and lick the owner cannot be mistaken for anything but "I'm really happy to see you."

## DO DOGS HAVE A SIXTH SENSE?

**!**

Though many believe dogs are telepathic, it is often merely their ability to hear distant sounds long before a human does—from up to four times as far away. Dogs will know the sound of their leader's car or their leader's footsteps as she or he walks up the driveway to the house, and will be ready and waiting by the front door. Dogs can also hear higher-pitched sounds, such as those emitted by bats or rodents. There are also many documented cases of dogs becoming agitated minutes before an earthquake.

# "Hey, that smells really interesting."

Another way a dog greets his owner—in fact, every other animal he meets—is by sniffing him. Though it varies from species to species, a dog's nose can be forty times more sensitive than a human's nose, and so a dog can distinguish between smells to a far greater degree.

Gundogs and sniffer dogs, such as springer spaniels, will often go straight for the crotch area of a human because that is where their scent is most intense and least masked by deodorants or soap. Such dogs are trained to react to smell, and they go right for it, no matter how embarrassing the consequences.

## THE STING ON THE NOSE, NOT THE TAIL

Sniffer dogs aren't used only to detect explosives or illegal drugs—their noses can be so sensitive that they can hunt out bumblebee nests. In Scotland, springer spaniels were used to survey the nests of wild bumblebees that were becoming extinct in the Hebridean islands. They were trained to sniff them out but not get too close when they found them.

# "You know, I'm sure I've smelled you before somewhere."

The greeting ritual of dogs is to sniff and be sniffed. Whereas humans put most of their recognition skills into eyesight, dogs need the confirmation of smell. This often results in both animals staying stock-still while they go about the important business. Knowing exactly how other dogs smell helps them figure out who's who in the marking process. When they go out on walks, they will come across these scents sprayed around the neighborhood and know just who's been where and how long ago.

Out on the streets, time, wind, and rain diminish the smell, but up close it's much easier to identify other dogs. In this picture, the greyhound is less excited to get to know the younger dog, who is eager to get to the point.

# "That's funny, they don't usually lock it."

Dogs learn by observation. They have to, because their mother has vital lessons to pass on to them. They need to see what she does and then copy her. Though some of it is instinctive, Border collies learn their craft by watching other dogs herd sheep. To be able to perform observed tasks, dogs need a brain that is sufficiently developed; however, they still have only half the learning ability of primates. This dog knows from watching its owner that a simple twist of the handle is enough to gain access to the house. The only problem is, the dogs hadn't expected the door to be locked.

## TEACHING AN OLD DOG . . .

Everyone knows the phrase "you can't teach an old dog new tricks," and it's true. This is partly due to the fact that, as dogs get older, their brains weigh less. An old dog has a brain that is 25 percent lighter than a younger dog's. The main reason for the inability to learn new tricks is that the nerve connections break down with age as the nerve cells contract. Also, as dogs get older, the messages that are sent along the nerves take longer to travel. With old dogs, it can take as much as four times longer for the nervous system to deliver a command from the brain to a muscle.

# "I'm not gonna blink." "I'm not gonna blink, either!"

Staring down a rival is one of the key tasks that needs to be accomplished to achieve top-dog status. These dogs know each other, and the confrontation isn't as full-on as it could be if they were strangers—especially in such close proximity. The tricolored Border collie has its tail and head held as high as possible in order to intimidate the other dog. The gaze of the collie is too much, and the sandy-colored dog has broken off and looked away, thus giving the collie a little victory. Notice that the dog to the collie's right isn't sure what is about to go down and so has remained very still to give the message that it is no threat and that the other two can just get on with it.

## ! DOMINANT BEHAVIOR

The biggest single behavioral problem in dogs is aggression, especially dominance aggression, where the dog begins to think it's top dog of the household, humans included. As a result, it starts to guard certain areas and will allow admission to some people in the house but not others. The situation comes about by letting a dog have its own way all the time—and though owners may think they are being laid-back and animal-friendly, they are actually creating a problem. Dogs need to know their place in the household's hierarchy.

# "Okay, maybe you are tougher."

Dogs don't want to risk serious injury by getting into fights they can't win. In many respects, dogs are a lot more pragmatic about this than humans. They will often get involved in play-fights with dogs of a similar size just to see who is more likely to come out on top should they do it for real. As part of the rough and tumble—normally in a group of dogs—they might occasionally try play-mounting another dog. This isn't a serious attempt to reproduce by a dog who has misread the signals. It's an opportunity to practice while getting one up on their playmates. Bitches will do the same with other bitches to remind them of their superior status.

**!**

## NOT WORTH A FIGHT

Fights only tend to get serious when the stakes are high. Food is no longer the reason for many dogfights. A serious clash of territory or the right to breed with a bitch in heat are the most powerful motivators for dogs to fight. While the number of reasons for dogs to compete has diminished, the propensity for dogs to fight has increased with so many dogs bred for guard duty.

# "Shut it, why don't you?"

Muzzle biting takes two forms in the dog world, as it does in the wolf world. First, there is the soft muzzle bite of the dominant dog over the submissive dog. Here, a mother shows just who is the boss by clamping her jaws gently over one of her pups who has been irritating her. It's a power trip; the puppy is definitely not in charge of this situation. The pups on page 30 are trying some muzzle "fencing," which is similar, like two swordsmen dueling, but neither can "outjaw" the other.

Muzzle biting using a hard bite is an aggressive move meant to put another dog firmly in its place.

## ! MASSIVE MASTIFF

The world's heaviest (and longest) dog ever recorded was an English mastiff named Zorba. In 1989, Zorba weighed a massive 341 pounds and was 10 feet long from nose to tail. The oldest dog on record was an Australian cattle dog named Bluey. In 1939, he was euthanized at the age of twenty-nine years and five months.

# "I'm tallest, so please be impressed!"

Dogs will try to block access to show that they are in charge and have superior status. However, in this situation, the dog on the left is standing over the other dog and is not being blocked. Instead he is trying to dominate the other dog by standing over him in what he hopes looks like a threatening manner. However, since they are both from the same litter, the dog on the right isn't taking this move too seriously at all and is turning to sniff him. Both dogs have their tails up in the alert, ready-for-action mode, so this could still turn nasty.

## AVOIDING AGGRESSION

The best way to keep dogs from assuming a dominant and aggressive role in the household is by catching it early. When your dog is still a puppy, it needs to be shown who is the boss. This means feeding it when you want to—not on demand. It also helps if owners can show they are able to make arbitrary decisions about a pup's environment by removing his toys, then returning them. Another key point is never to let a puppy get away with aggressive moves like nipping or play-mounting. Some owners find it difficult to be a spoilsport, but it is necessary.

# "Look at this—I am a very fierce and powerful hunter."

Another bit of dog drama that may be interpreted as "just playing" is the crouching threat of attack. What may look like two dogs playing a game is actually one dog saying to another: "This could happen to you if you're not careful." The top dog will crouch in readiness to spring at the other dog but will not carry through the full attack and just fake a forward movement to put the other dog on edge. It gives the clear message that it knows how to fight—and would if provoked. In many ways, groups of dogs aren't that different from gangs of youths.

## CHILDREN BEWARE

Dogs can be aggressive because they are fearful. Pups that haven't been properly socialized by being introduced to children and adults can be very fearful when they encounter this "strange new species." The reason children get bitten so much is that they haven't learned to read the signals of a wary and fearful dog and assume it is going to be as loving and playful as the last one they encountered.

# "Hi, and get a whiff of this!"

An erect tail is a sign that a dog is confident and potentially aggressive. It wants the whole world to know its smell. It is alert and ready for action, and could be out to challenge another dog. It would be unusual for a dog to hold its tail upright without the stimulus of another dog to impress. Holding the tail upright can be accompanied by a dog raising itself up to its full height, as seen on page 59. A further stage is when a dog raises its hackles (the fur on the back of its neck) to make itself look as big as possible.

These dogs both have erect tails and are meeting on equal terms. Even though they are looking at each other directly, it will last just a few seconds before they agree to move on and sniff other, more rewarding areas.

## TINY TROUBLEMAKERS

One reason for dogs to be fearful of children is that children are excitable and run and move unpredictably. Dogs may also harbor grudges against children. If they have reacted in the past and were reprimanded as a result, they begin to associate children with the fear of another scolding—so children are seen as nothing but small troublemakers.

# "Me first, me first, me first!"

Dogs like to be first in line—like squabbling siblings who have to be first to get the ice cream or be first on the swings—and pick their spot, so status-conscious dogs like to score little victories over their rivals in the pack, be it an all-human pack or an all-dog pack.

Allowing dogs to always be first can go to their heads. On walks, when they're straining to read all the messages

on a particularly "well-written" fire hydrant or tree, it's useful to show just who is in charge and keep them moving.

In the wild, a wolf can exert its authority by controlling where other members of the pack go. In the house, dogs may play an access game where they try and keep members of the family—or other dogs—from getting past them. Though on the surface it may seem like fun and games, the dog is trying to win these small challenges to enhance his status. Getting status within the pack is easier done by small, petty challenges than risking a head-on confrontation that could leave it injured or humbled in front of others. Owners often miss the significance of these little dares.

### BAA, RAM, EWE

The best way to train your dog not to attack another animal is to introduce it to that animal at an early age. Dogs raised with cats and rabbits will rarely chase or attack them. Shepherds apply the same technique with sheepdogs. They want their dogs to be aggressive at times and to push around stubborn old rams and ewes, but they don't want their dogs to attack the livestock. Thus Border collies are brought up in close contact with sheep.

# "I'm as soft as a marshmallow, I am."

This puppy has rolled over onto its back and for all the world it looks like it wants its tummy tickled. It might, but that's not the reason the puppy is on its back. By rolling over and exposing its belly, it has shown that it is vulnerable and no threat. It is demonstrating one of the typically submissive acts it has learned while part of the litter. Dogs use this move to get them out of situations where they feel an attack might be imminent. In this case, the puppy is performing for its mom, who uses the opportunity to sniff that all is well.

In the home, an owner is not going to attack her pet, but she might scold it for some misdemeanor. The rolling-over display is a "puppy act," showing that the dog is weak and powerless and will accept the owner's dominance without question.

## ! LESSONS PUPPIES LEARN

All the acts that demonstrate submission are present in puppyhood: tail between legs, eyes averted, rolling onto its back, lying on its side, urinating, and staying still while an aggressor circles or play-mounts them.

# "You're really, really great."

Showing a submissive roll-over position to a dominant dog who has approached is fine, but how does the lower-status dog approach a dominant dog? He wants the dominant dog to know that he accepts its status. Walking directly toward the top dog could be seen as confrontational, so he has to let the top dog know things are cool and that he's still the boss. The lower-status dog conveys this with another puppylike gesture. Puppies beg for food by jumping up and licking at the bitch's mouth. The lower-status dog will imitate this by going down into a crouch and then coming up to attempt a lick—acting out the puppy role to show that it is no threat to the top dog and accepts its status.

# "I'm not stronger than you."

Another act of submission by dogs that is frequently misunderstood is the raised paw.

When a dog raises its paw instinctively, it is not trying to say, "Hello, pleased to meet you!" (The nose in the groin can do that.) The raised paw is an act of submission. Dogs will do it between themselves, not just with their owners or members of the family. If the raised paw is combined with lowered eyes and a lowered head, the submission is all the more meaningful.

## BAD DOG!

The need to physically punish a dog in training should hardly ever be necessary, since there are so many psychological tools at an owner's disposal. An owner can reprimand bad behavior in a dog by staring at him while letting him know he's a "bad dog!" Given a dog's ability to pick up on human body language, he will get the message. If the dog's gaze back at the owner is averted, it's not because he's not listening.

# "Please don't hurt me, I'm scar-r-r-ed!"

Everyone knows the phrase "he went away with his tail between his legs," meaning that a loser in a contest wasn't just beaten, he was soundly beaten and retreated almost in shame. The tail between the legs is a submissive pose meant to show other members of the pack that it is not a threat and is of a low social status. By lowering the tail, the dog is covering up his anal glands that waft his scent out into the world and thus preventing others from sniffing out exactly who he is. It's the equivalent of a person leaving a court building in shame after being convicted and hiding his face from the waiting cameras by covering it with a coat or newspaper.

**!**

### TAIL TABOO

The raising and lowering of tails can be witnessed in wolf packs. Wolves in the pack will lower their tails when they are with the pack leader. Keeping it high would be confrontational.

# "This is strange and I don't like it!"

Barking is a dog's way of saying "Something's not right" or "Watch out, I've detected something." Dogs can bark for all sorts of reasons. When a dog is wary of strangers, it will bark to call for backup and also to try and scare them away, usually with a series of short, sharp, urgent barks and a rush forward.

Of course, if the first rush doesn't work, they'll back up and try another rush. It's all bluff. Barking means that a dog is not going to attack, because when a dog has decided to attack, it stays silent.

### IT'S NOT A SNARL, IT'S A SMILE

When a dog opens its mouth to show its teeth, it doesn't *always* want to take a chunk out of your leg. The dog "smile" is the canine equivalent of a dopey grin, but because dogs can't grin with their mouths shut, all those teeth can make it look like it's a threat. In order to tell if your dog is smiling and not snarling, you have to see the rest of the body posture and the look in his eyes. The dog smile is silent and the body is relaxed, not straining. In fact, it's just like a pant but without the heavy breathing.

# "What about me?"

Small dogs often have high-pitched, "yappy" barks. And because they tend to be companion dogs—unlike large dogs that guard, hunt, track, or stay outside apart from the family—they expect a lot of human contact. So small dogs use their barks to attract attention, like spoiled children who don't get their way. The message is still the same: "Something's not right"—but in this case, it is simply a feeling of being ignored.

To emphasize this need for attention, the pup on the right is standing up on his hind legs to try and make eye contact with someone at a much higher level. He has also learned that this kind of "begging action" evokes a warm and fuzzy response from his owners.

## FROM 20 TO 700 BREEDS

It's been estimated that there were no more than twenty distinct dog breeds in Europe during the Middle Ages. The rapid expansion in breeds since then has been a result of imports from around the world and intensive selective breeding, with dog breeders pursuing the perfect dog for specific jobs and purposes.

# "Which way did he say?"

Sheepdogs are unusual in that they have a remarkable ability to round up animals, and also that they can respond to audible signals from a shepherd. Most dogs will learn spoken commands much quicker if they are accompanied by a hand signal or are physically moved into a position. These commands—"sit," "lie down," and "heel"—are typical for most basic dog-training courses. With experience, the dog will learn to respond to the spoken command without the need for the hand gesture. Puppies can be trained from eight weeks onward, and owners should remember to make their training commands firm and consistent so that there is no doubt in the puppy's mind about what he is being asked to do.

## ! TOP DOGS

The most popular breeds of dog in the United States are the Labrador retriever, golden retriever, German shepherd, beagle, and dachshund. The Labrador retriever is also the most popular dog in the UK and Canada.

# "I am so very frightening!"

Dogs would sooner frighten off other dogs than get into a fight they could lose—so the growl is used as a device to say "Beware!" There are two stages of aggression with dogs before an attack is launched. First, there is the bark: "I don't like you." "This is strange." "Where's my owner?" "Go away, I've got some tough friends around the corner!"

If this doesn't work, dogs will move to a growl. They realize the aggressor is not going to be scared off by a bark and is too close now, so the growl says: "I could attack at any moment, so back off right now." Dogs can also use the growl to warn humans that they've made too much contact, are touching a place of pain, or are making the dog anxious by their touch or proximity.

## ALL THE PRESIDENTS' DOGS

There are many tales of U.S. presidents' dogs. Franklin D. Roosevelt is said to have spent $15,000 to have a destroyer return to the Aleutian Islands and retrieve his Scottie, Fala, who had been left behind. Fala was an honorary army private. Teddy Roosevelt's pit bull, Pete, once caused a diplomatic incident by ripping the trousers of the French ambassador. President Lyndon Johnson owned a stray dog named Yuki who was rescued by Johnson's daughter Luci from a Texas gas station.

# "I have some very sharp teeth, and I'm not afraid to use them."

The eyes are fixed and the stare is hard. The lips are drawn back to reveal the teeth, which could be used at a moment's notice. The bluff is gone now and the real threat is there. It is the preparation to fight: a show of strength from which it is very difficult for the dog to back down. Dogs that snarl at each other usually fight if they can get at each other. Humans have the ability to back away from a dog in such a situation, but if they do, they must make that retreat obvious. Otherwise a dog might interpret it as a sly form of attack. Take it slow and steady.

# "It's mine."

Dogs have a certain way of looking you in the eye as if to say "Back off, this is mine." It's not as extreme a reaction as the bone-hogging snarl. Approach a dog that has a hold of a nicely shaped stick or a prized possession, and they will stop what they are doing, become quite still, and give you the "It's mine" look.

### CALMING FEARS

A sustained fearful reaction in dogs can become a phobia and needs to be treated by a trained animal behaviorist. Dogs can develop phobias to anything that routinely causes fear in them. One phobia that is difficult to cure is the fear of visiting the vet. This is due to the vet being associated with pain, bright lights, and being held down in an uncomfortable position, not to mention all the strange smells and sounds associated with the building itself. An initial trip to the vet for a very mild treatment or just an introductory visit is a great way to ease the anxiety of future visits.

# "This is way too interesting to leave stuck in the garbage."

Dogs in the wild will hunt in packs for larger animals, they will hunt alone for smaller prey they can bring down themselves, or they will scavenge for leftovers from more wasteful eaters. In the home, dogs are given their one or two meals a day, and canine obesity is more of a problem than underfeeding. Yet they still love to hunt and scavenge. The dog that tries to haul something out of the garbage is responding to an ancient urge. Just as smelly objects are there to be rolled in, dogs (and cats for that matter) can't resist the strong smell of food calling to them.

## NOT-SO-FUSSY EATERS

One of the reasons that dogs are happy to eat meat of questionable taste is their much-less-fussy taste buds. While humans are thought to have around 9,000 taste buds, dogs are estimated to have less than 2,000.

# "When's my next meal coming?"

One contributing factor to dogs who feel the need to scavenge food is meal timing. Even animals as small as fish get used to being fed at regular times. The busy schedules of pet owners often means they are not home at the same time every day. If a dog becomes unsure of when its next meal is coming, then it is more likely to scavenge, so a dog that regularly attacks the garbage or gets caught eating other dogs' food is saying "There's not enough" or "I'm not sure I'm going to get fed tonight."

## WOLFING IT DOWN

Dogs eat quickly on their own, but in groups they eat even quicker. This is because of the inbred competitive element within them to get resources that other dogs might want. Feeding dogs in groups will actually provoke them into eating more than usual. Vets use this technique to get dogs who are off their food to take an interest. Similarly, when new fish are introduced into an aquarium, they can be stimulated into feeding competitively by putting them with a voracious eater.

# "It's my bone—that's the rule!"

Dogs can be very possessive over bones or big chunks of meat that they have "won." Even seemingly good-tempered dogs can get snarly if an approach is made to take their prize—such as a meaty chew or a big, juicy bone.

Part of this goes back to wolf-pack behavior. In wolf packs, if one of the weaker, lower-status wolves captures a big, meaty chunk for itself, the higher-status wolves or pack leader will not take it from him. Similarly, dogs believe that when they win something, it's theirs—that's the law—and will even defend it against dogs they would normally be afraid of.

45

# "A little treat for later."

Dogs have no problem eating decomposing meat. The irony is that so many spoiled dogs are eating prime cuts when they'd be just as happy with a piece of rotting flesh. (Though, obviously, the dental hygiene isn't so good in this situation—you don't want a slobbery "welcome home" lick from your dog twenty minutes after he's polished off half a rotting rabbit!)

So, faced with an oversupply of food, dogs may try to hide some of it, as their wolf ancestors did in the wild. And that involves finding a suitable location or burying it. Like so many other doggy traits, it's not a failure on the part of the owner—it's a little bit of the wolf showing through. Why do they often bury bones or chews? Because burying each little piece of canned or dry dog food is nearly impossible!

## CHEWING GRASS

As with cats, there is no fully established theory as to why dogs eat grass. Some eat grass to make themselves vomit—though dogs aren't nearly as susceptible to hair balls as their feline friends. Some dogs chew grass for the sheer pleasure of chewing it and because it's right there in front of them. Given the choice of grass or a dog-chew, though, there is no competition.

# "It's playtime!"

The signal from dogs that it's time to play is one of the easiest to recognize. It's called the "play bow," and dogs will put their paws and elbows on the ground, lowering their front half while leaving their rumps high in the air, as though they are bowing. Dogs will use this technique with other dogs as well as with their owners to invite play. They may even want to show how playful they are by doing it as an introduction.

## ! IT'S A VISION THING

Dogs have very good vision at a distance, poor vision up close, excellent awareness of movement, and terrific peripheral vision. This explains why they spot things a long way away, yet when it comes to spotting a stationary ball right in front of their nose, they go right past it.

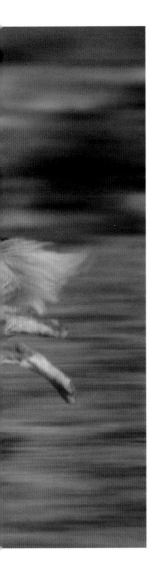

## "I'll catch it, easy."

Another easy-to-recognize "let's play" signal is the offered
stick or toy. A dog will drop an object, most likely a stick
or a ball, in front of his owner in an attempt to get him to
throw it. Once the object is dropped, he'll retreat two or
three paces with his eyes fixed pointedly at the object.
It's classic learned behavior, though the part owners
sometimes misunderstand is when dogs want to wrestle,
not fetch. Instead of allowing the owner to pick up the
object, the dog wants to pick it up again and simulate a
puppyhood wrestling battle, when it would battle for top-
dog status by being the one that got the stick. In adulthood
it's a play battle, reenacted for fun. However, if a dog wants
to perpetually hold on and resists all attempts by the
owner to take the stick, then it's another little victory, a sign
that the dog may think it's the leader of the family pack.

# "Let me at him!"

The pack instinct to chase is never far away from dogs, and while cats will never work up a sweat unless they have to, dogs are only too willing to chase, chase, chase. Chasing can be a problem when dogs see runners and bicyclists as irresistible. In more serious cases, dogs will chase livestock, so owners should always keep them on a leash when livestock are near. Two dogs together are emboldened and will try things that one dog wouldn't risk alone. And so the professional dog walker who negotiates the neighborhood with five leashes can sometimes run into a problem when one of her charges wants to . . . well . . . charge.

# "What's that behind me?"

Dogs that chase their tails show the classic symptoms of understimulation. They're bored. What might look like an amusing trait can actually be a worrying one. Dogs are not having a little fun: "What's that behind me? There it is again! Whoa, it's still there!" Dogs who chase their tails are really telling their owners, "I'm so bored, this is what I've been reduced to!"

People may think their dog is just a little bit crazy. Well, it is—stir crazy, with nothing much to do. Dogs need to be stimulated and exercised.

## BARD DOG

The poet and playwright William Shakespeare was a dog lover and supposedly a great admirer of basset hounds. The only dog that appears in a Shakespeare play is Crab, who has a role in *The Two Gentlemen of Verona*.

# "Go on, pass it to me, I'm open!"

Kids and dogs have many things in common, and one of them is an oversupply of energy. So it's only natural that the family dog gets involved in all kinds of chasing games in the park or around the backyard with the kids. However, some children can get very frightened by dogs, so it's important that dogs know that while they can instigate chasing games with their own "pack" of children, children from other packs might not be so eager to join in. Limiting the chasing games to thrown toys can avoid lots of potential problems—though the temptation to race after any Frisbee they see in the park can never be ruled out.

## DOG-TASTIC

There are approximately 68 million dogs in the United States, ranging from mongrels to pedigree pooches that are shown at the annual Westminster Dog Show. Approximately 36 percent of homes in America have dogs as pets, and about five million puppies are born every year.

# "You're not going to win this one!"

Dogs also love playing chasing games among themselves. While they shouldn't be allowed to play chase with children from "another pack," they have enough canine judgment to figure out if another dog is up for the chase, especially if one of them gives a perfunctory play bow. It's estimated that 98 percent of dogs don't use up their potential of energy in a day.

**!**

## VISUAL RANGE

A dog's vision is different from ours. We see sharper images, but dogs see movement better—and while we can see in color, dogs have a narrower spectrum that gives them very good twilight vision. Dogs have a visual range of 250 degrees, whereas the human range is 180 degrees.

# "Kill the toy!"

Another big difference between the calorie-conserving cat and the run-all-day dog is what they do when they capture their prey. Whereas a cat will be tempted to play around with it for maximum fun, the dog is merciful and dispatches its victims quickly. The grab with the jaws and the twist and shake that dogs give to rubber toys is a reenactment of what it would do in real life if it caught a rabbit or bird. In Europe, fox hunters and hare coursers still witness this powerful end to a dog's hunting drive when they pick up the fox and shake it. This is one reason why hunting dogs should be given prey substitutes to keep them stimulated. While many people shun the idea of hunting for pleasure in the twenty-first century, terriers that catch vermin are still regarded as essential. Giving terrier pups an array of squeaky rubber vermin to "kill" will strengthen their neck and jaw muscles if they have to go out and do the real thing.

# "I don't care if there's no meaty goodness in this squeaky peg—my teeth are lovin' it."

Once they have killed the squeaky toy, the next logical step for a dog is to chew it to pieces. In the wild, wolves and pack dogs devour their prey for food. With all meals provided for the domestic dog, chewing their "catch" is an enjoyable hobby. Again, it is the instinct of the hunter to keep the jaws exercised and the teeth sharp. And while he might feel guilty about chewing up an object he found in the house or backyard, this is his—he won it. Humans love popping bubble wrap; dogs can't resist chewing. What's the point of having jaws that could—if necessary—lever muscle away from bone if all they do is crunch biscuits?

One cautionary note: always make sure the toy you give your dog is too big to be swallowed.

# "Whoa! That really made me jump."

Puppy play doesn't always sort out the leader of the pack, but it does help them hone their running, jumping, coordination, and social skills. They find out who's the strongest, the most stubborn, the most easily bullied—who is mentally tough and who buckles into submissive behavior at the first sign of aggression. Rough and tumble

can be enjoyed for what it is, but it will get serious very soon. The hierarchy in a wolf pack or wild dog pack will change over time as top dogs become old dogs and new challengers take over, but dogs are still able to move up and down in social status within their own pack even if they're not after the top spot.

# "Go on, it's your turn to play the attacker."

Dogs who haven't learned to play can be difficult to deal with. Young dogs may also be too scared to join in the play and, like good youth workers, the older dogs will adopt strategies to try and get them to join in the fun. A deliberate and overtly submissive act, such as rolling on the floor, by a high-status adult can put the younger ones at ease. Similarly, smaller dogs will be wary of joining in play with a much larger animal, scared that they might have misread the signals. So the big dog has to make it very obvious that it's playtime. Huge Irish wolfhounds must have to do quite a bit of rolling around to get a good game going.

## ! GONE TO THE DOGS

An American Animal Hospital Association poll revealed some interesting statistics about owners' devotion to their dogs. They found that 70 percent of people sign their pet's name on greeting cards and 33 percent of them talk to their dogs on the phone. It has been estimated that one million dogs in the United States are the principal beneficiary in their owner's will.

# "Let's go crazy!"

One signal inviting others to play is when a dog performs a whirling dervish act. It will bounce across the grass, jump in the air, twist, run some more, and generally act like it is going crazy. However, the small barks of delight and the sheer joy that it is exhibiting make it clear that it is excited to be out and about. These exuberant displays are typically performed by energetic dogs that have been cooped up inside. Some people think this is a sign of a dog getting agitated about having fleas or other parasites attacking its fur, but it's not.

Hunters used to employ "tolling dogs" to perform a dance that would attract curious wild duck—and then shoot them. The ducks, that is.

## AND NOW THE MOOS

Ironically, cows will perform a more muted version of this leap of joy when they are let out on the grass for the first time after a winter of being kept indoors.

# "I really dig this."

Dogs dig for four reasons—to hide food, to uncover prey, to escape, or simply for the joy of digging.

Dogs don't mind a bit of dirt on their food—they have powerful digestive juices to deal with this. The drive to hide food comes from their desire to be in control of their food supply in an unpredictable world. As with so many squirrel caches, most of it is never dug up again.

Not surprisingly, dogs prefer to do their burying in private. If interrupted in their burying attempts, they will stop, only to continue somewhere else later on—when the coast is clear. They don't realize that the heap of earth in the middle of a beautifully manicured lawn is a bit of a giveaway. Toys and balls aren't safe from burying, either.

The dog on the right is digging for pleasure and to keep cool. Through its sensitive paws, it has figured out that the layer of shingle below the surface is really cool, so it's chilling out on the wet stones it has uncovered.

> **!**
>
> ### MALE vs. FEMALE
>
> Unlike their owners, male dogs carry more of their body weight as fat than do female dogs. So, not surprisingly, male dogs will eat more than females.

# "Just practicing."

One of the most popular breeds of dogs in the United States is the dachshund, which was bred to dig out badgers. However, many other breeds of dogs dig to uncover prey, such as rabbits, or flush out small mammals for humans to dispose of. Owners of terriers have even seen their pets going through the motions of digging and nosing imaginary earth around inside the house.

**!**

## SEA DOGS

There are documentary records of dogs that both survived and went down with the *Titanic* in 1912. Henry Harper's Pekinese, Su Yan Set, and Pomeranians owned by Margaret Hays and Elizabeth Rothschild survived along with their owners. A French bulldog named Gamin de Pycombe and its owner, Robert Daniel, were lost. Colonel John Jacob Astor and his two Airedales were also lost in the disaster.

# "I'll just flatten this 'grass' down."

Nobody likes to sleep on a lumpy bed, so why should dogs be any different? When a dog gets into its basket or bed, it will turn around ritually to iron out the lumps. It's a trait inherited from the wild, where dogs would turn around to flatten grass or earth before they went to sleep. Another trait inherited from the wild (and shared with cats) is their love of dens—a sleeping place that has a secure, "tucked-away" feel about it, such as under a table, in a corner, or behind a sofa.

## ! DOG TIRED

About 80 percent of a dog's sleeping time is spent in slow-wave sleep. The rest is occupied by REM (rapid eye movement) sleep, which helps restore the neurotransmitters in the brain. Puppies will sleep anywhere from fifteen to twenty hours a day, even up to the age of twelve weeks.

# "Okay, I'll save the fight with the toy for later."

The average dog will sleep longer than a human—anything from ten to fourteen hours per day. But dogs don't necessarily sleep at the same times. Once it gets into a routine of taking its major sleep period at the same time as the "human pack," things will settle down fine, but it's useful for puppies to have some kind of quiet nighttime stimulus, such as a small toy to play with, should they wake up in the middle of the night. Otherwise everyone can get disturbed. Puppies often sleep in bouts of four to five hours, so giving them something to keep them occupied in the wee hours is a shrewd move.

# "Actually, I'm not totally asleep."

Dognapping—grabbing fifteen minutes of sleep in every two hours—is also known as polyphasic sleeping. Unlike monophasic sleeping, where there is only one sleep period every twenty-four hours, polyphasic sleeping allows for much more time spent awake in each twenty-four-hour cycle. A lot of great men, such as Leonardo da Vinci and Thomas Edison, were believed to have been dognappers. This Weimaraner pup was so comfortable in front of the camera that it managed to grab some quick shut-eye.

## THE FEAR FACTOR

Between eight to ten weeks of age, puppies go through their first "fear imprint" period, when the world becomes a nastier place. It's important that puppies are not exposed to potentially frightening or painful experiences during this period, because the effects can imprint themselves in the puppy's memory. It's usually best not to move a puppy to a new home during this time, due to all the upheaval and confusion that it entails.

# "This is close enough, I suppose."

Dogs can be demanding, and many will want to sleep on their owner's bed. It's a throwback to puppyhood, where all the puppies snuggled in and found a place with their mother. With most dogs experiencing the life of a domestic puppy—no hunting, no sexual activity, and all meals provided by their pseudo parents—it's a natural assumption for them to make. Allowing a dog to sleep on its owner's bed is a dangerous precedent, because even if they are Yorkies or Chihuahuas, there will be times when it is impractical for them to do so, which can spark howls of rejection and barks of abandonment.

The biggest behavioral problem outside of dog aggression is learned attention seeking. It can be quite difficult to wean a dog from sleeping in its owner's bed if it was allowed to do so as a puppy.

**!**

### SPACE DOGS

The first animal to travel into space was a small mongrel dog named Laika, who orbited the earth in the Russian Sputnik 2 in 1957. Laika was found wandering the streets of Moscow. Her "backup cosmonauts" were Albina and Mushka.

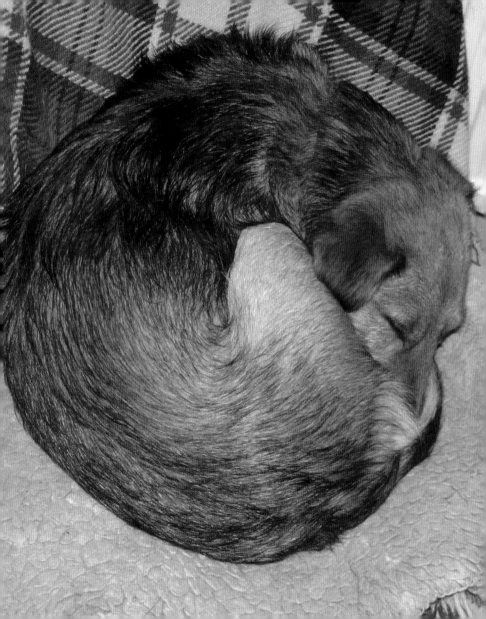

# "Looks like I'm stuck here."

As a pack animal, dogs feel part of the family, so even if they can't sleep on the bed, they'd like to sleep in the bedroom. Or, if not in the bedroom, on the landing outside or at least in the house with the rest of the "pack." Though dogs can learn to live in an outside kennel, the feeling of being inside and secure with the rest of the pack is best. They cannot understand why they would be segregated so far away from the rest of their family. Sleeping outside can also induce fear in smaller dogs, who remain wary about a threat that may lie on just the other side of the fence.

### VERY OLD DOGS

The earliest evidence of a domesticated dog comes from around 12,000 BC. A burial site in Israel revealed the skeleton of a woman holding a small puppy. The oldest American dog breed is the American foxhound. They date back to 1650, when Robert Brooke introduced a pack of hunting hounds from England.

## "Zzzzzzzzzzzzzzzzz."

While dogs are sleeping, they will occasionally twitch their paws, quiver their body, whimper, moan, or even growl. They're dreaming. During the night—just like humans—they will have phases of light sleep and deeper REM sleep. It is during these periods that they dream. But whether they're dreaming of cats not chased, Frisbees not caught, or bones that will be forever lost, nobody knows. However, it is good advice to let sleeping dogs lie.

## A BASSET'S ASSETS

The basset was bred in England for hunting small game such as rabbits and pheasants. Its long ears help stir up and hold the scent for their sensitive noses to smell and follow. The folds of skin under the chin—the dewlap—are used to trap and hold the scent as well. Wrinkles around the head and face also help keep the scent. With short legs and a steady pace, they are ideal for slow tracking, allowing huntsmen with guns to follow on foot.

# "What a relief to find this place."

Humans sweat, but the only way a dog can cool down, apart from finding a shady spot, is to pant. The only place a dog has sweat glands is on its feet. The action of water evaporating off the tongue takes heat away from the dog and helps cool the blood. The more the tongue is exposed out of the mouth, the more water that can be evaporated, and hence the cooler it becomes.

This is partly the reason that dogs fare so badly when they are left in cars on hot days with no ventilation. The dog may try and lose heat through its tongue but finds it increasingly difficult because the air in the car gets more and more humid the more it pants.

**!**

## SLEEPLESS IN SAN DIEGO

The heavy coats worn by dogs are a vestige of their ancestry and their origin in colder climates. Too much heat was never usually the problem; too much cold was the killer. It is only from the twentieth century that dogs have had it so good. In the modern global economy, families often have to be professionally mobile, exchanging work locations in San Diego and Seattle or Phoenix and New York. The heat ranges between such locations are huge, putting stress on a domestic dog that may live through many changes during its twelve to fifteen years.

# 67

## "I know I'm in the way, but . . ."

Whereas cats are masters at finding the sunniest spots, hot dogs specialize in finding the coolest drafts. So if a dog sits itself down right in the middle of a doorway, it's not trying to get underfoot, it's trying to keep its temperature down. However, there can be other factors involved, too. Dogs like to know the comings and goings of the "pack," and a breeze can bring interesting scents with it. Most importantly, the dog can control access while sitting in the middle of a doorway.

# "Whoa! Scent overload!"

Dogs get very excited about car rides. They get new sights and new smells, and there's often a park at the end of the trip; sometimes they get to hang out of a window and cool down. The biggest rush for a dog, though, is the tidal wave of exciting new smells coming their way. In fact, so many smells come at them so quickly, it's difficult to make sense of them all. With a nose that's forty times more sensitive than that of a human, it's a sensory overload. Often you will see dogs absolutely transfixed as they hang out of a car window—and that is because it's like a human trying to watch a video on fast-forward.

## OFF TO THE RACES

Most domestic dogs are able to reach speeds of around 20 mph when running flat out. However, greyhounds are the speedsters of the canine world—some are able to reach a speed of almost 40 mph.

# "I might as well now that I'm here."

Marking with urine is not just a pleasant diversion for dogs to show that they've passed by; for males it's a bid for territorial dominance. Male dogs will lift their legs at frequent intervals on a walk, especially when they've smelled another male's recent visit to a tree or lamppost. Like posters in a popular spot, they plaster their scent on top of the old one so that theirs is read next. Sometimes dogs will become so active that they stop and mark too often and run out of urine. It doesn't stop them from lifting their legs, though, even if they have no "message" to leave. Bitches will also mark when doing their rounds, as this female is demonstrating, though never as regularly as males.

## NOTHING TO BE SNIFFED AT

Male dogs make better sniffers than female dogs because they are genetically programmed to analyze the scent of others as part of their territory marking.

# "This one's easy to read."

Dogs prefer to leave their mark against objects with strong verticals, such as trees, lampposts, or corners of buildings, for various reasons. These are specific route points. If dogs were to mark along the ground, it would necessitate other dogs trailing along with their noses permanently on the floor. Worse, the scents would be tramped on by humans and other animals and then easily rinsed away by rainfall. By lifting a leg against an upright object, they can mark at nose level to other dogs, making their scents far more noticeable. What's more, very few other types of scents are applied at that level, so the dogs' scents will stay undiluted and pure, and won't get washed off so much in the rain.

## PUTTING DOWN A MARKER

Marking varies through a dog's life. If your dog is an avid marker, though, it doesn't necessarily mean he (or occasionally she) is out to prove his dominance. Nervous dogs will mark on top of another dog's scent to get rid of it. It is the old "posting technique" where one poster pastes his flyer on top of the last one: "Read mine, not his!" A nervous dog's anxiety is reduced by his ability to mark on top of another dog's scent.

# "Wow, this smell is really interesting."

Like a veteran wine taster with a sophisticated palette, a dog's ability to analyze the aroma of another dog's scent is prodigious. In fact, a dog's skill of identification is much greater than a human's. The composition of urine, its freshness, the sex of the animal, and even the social status of the animal can be determined by careful sniffing. And if a particular smell is interesting but faint, there is a special technique dogs can use to enhance the experience. They will use sensory cells at the top of their mouth—usually devoted to taste—and will draw breath in with a motion involving chattering teeth. These three dogs have been stopped in their tracks by a particularly alluring smell. It's the carcass of a dead animal, lying not far below this cliff-top path.

## TRACING SCENTS

Until scientific equipment became more advanced at the beginning of the twenty-first century, dogs were used to detect minute quantities of a substance that were so dilute, they could not be measured in a laboratory.

# "I'm really proud of this one."

It sounds a bit like an avant-garde European artist, but dogs—after they've left a poop in the park or on the sidewalk—like to draw attention to their work. Rich with scent, it is their own artistic creation that they want the world to see and know who has passed by! To draw attention to it, they will scratch the ground nearby to show that it has been disturbed and that there is something significant on display for other dogs to smell. It's a habitual thing, and dogs will even be seen trying to paw the ground on hard urban surfaces as well as soft earth and grass in the backyard. Their wolf counterparts go much further than this. They will mark the ground up to three feet away as if to underline their "statement" in a territory that stretches for miles rather than yards.

No doubt, dogs are mortified when they see that as soon as they have produced their objet d'art, it gets scooped into a plastic bag and deposited into the next trash can in the park.

# "Now if I can pull this board off with my teeth . . ."

The drive to reproduce is great among unaltered dogs and can lead owners into desperate measures to keep their dogs in one place. You can hardly blame them. Bitches go into heat two times a year, while a male is ready to procreate at a moment's notice. And while the dog will go to great lengths—traveling huge distances if he picks up the faintest scent—to find his bitch, the bitch is also anxious to find a mate. It's often recommended that owners allow their bitches to go into heat once before having them spayed. One week into that season and they will be very anxious to get out to where the boys are.

## IRRESISTIBLE

Male dogs can smell the pheromones a bitch produces from three miles away—so it's easy to imagine the potential number of suitors in a three-mile radius. Owners who want to keep their dogs from wandering off should have them neutered. The lack of male hormones flooding through a dog's body will also reduce his levels of aggression. Aggression toward people and other dogs is by far the single biggest behavioral problem in canines.

# "No mistaking the signals from this one."

When a bitch goes into heat, she becomes restless, wanders around, drinks a lot, and urinates more often. Male dogs pick up the signals when she marks and want to get to her; however, the bitch will act moody and aggressive until she is ready to ovulate. A bitch will not lift her tail if she is not ready to be mounted and may attack impatient males who can't wait to get going. She'll sit down or spin around to prevent being mounted. However, when she is ready, she will lift her tail up and strut her legs so that the male is left with little doubt as to what's available.

## ! MAKING YOUR POINT

An appropriate punishment for a dog is to leave him alone. The minute a dog misbehaves, the owner goes out of the room and leaves him alone. Being pack animals, a dog thrives on being with the owner, not without the owner. It needs to be done the instant the behavior happens so that the dog gets to learn that his behavior is the cause of the owner's sudden absence.

# "How was it for you?"

**75**

After dogs have mated, they remain bonded together from between ten minutes to over an hour in some cases. They cannot physically separate themselves, and any attempts to undo this "tie" will result in short-term pain. Actually disentangling themselves is practically impossible because of this genital lock. The reason is that fertilization by male dogs is a three-stage process, and while humans can reproduce with just one ejaculation, dogs need three different types to complete their work. Nature has managed to devise a process where they cannot separate from each other with the job only half done, so the dog and the bitch remain bonded together for some time.

**!**

### TWICE A YEAR

Dogs may owe a lot to their wolf ancestry, but over time they have become more fertile. Whereas a female wolf comes into season only once a year, almost all dogs except the basenji come into season twice a year.

# "What's going to happen next?"

Dogs have many human traits, and yawning when they are anxious is one of them. In tense situations where there is a steady buildup of anxiety—such as before an exam or a meeting, or when going onstage—humans will yawn. Some people interpret this as a completely laid-back personality, so calm he or she is almost comatose. It's not the case at all, and it's the same with dogs. Dogs may yawn if they come under pressure and are unsure what they should do next. In the same way that a dog with a wagging tail isn't necessarily pleased to see you, so a yawning dog is not necessarily tired and his yawn could be communicating anxiety. Whereas one of these collie pups is happy to sit and pose, the other is yawning from anxiety.

### AN ANXIOUS WAIT

Many dogs suffer from separation anxiety, the fear of being left alone. The most likely dogs to suffer are those who make a big fuss of their owners whenever they return and then follow them like a shadow, i.e., dogs that show little independence.

# "Why is he staring at me?"

Another telltale clue that a dog is feeling ill at ease or on edge is the flick of the tongue. It's a quick nose lick, a quick dart of the tongue that gives the game away. This may often be seen in context with acts of submission when dogs are desperate to impress upon another dog that they are below its status and pose no threat. They may carry out these acts with human pack members who hold higher status, too. Dogs hate being stared at because it is part of the process that top dogs use to establish dominance. If, without realizing it, you have been staring at a dog, you may find him licking his nose or yawning.

## NOISE ANNOYS

One of the tricks that animal trainers use to stop a dog's bad behavior—such as detouring on walks to scavenge for food—is to use a loud, distracting noise. The second the dog misbehaves, a can full of beads is dropped onto the sidewalk to make an alarming noise. Dogs learn to stop straining at the leash and avoid the rattle can.

# "Nope, not interested."

While yawning, licking their noses, or wagging their tails may indicate that dogs are nervous and uncomfortable, there are various strategies they have developed to cope with it. Dogs are deft exponents of body language, and those they are wary of (that they don't view as potential aggressors) can be given the doggy cold shoulder—i.e., they'll turn their back to them. It may be as simple as the head turned imperiously away, as if to say "Not listening, not interested." This puppy is coping with the situation by turning his back to the camera, but curiosity got the better of him and he's been lured into looking back by the sound of a squeaky toy.

### FACT

The basenji is very close to its wolf ancestor in that it comes into season only once a year and very rarely barks—though it does give a basenji-specific "baroo." They were discovered helping tribesmen round up game in the African Congo in 1895. Their African name means "dog of the savages."

# "Maybe they won't notice if I quietly slink off."

An offending dog's hurried retreat might give another dog or a human the idea that they are in a position of advantage over the offending dog. Worse, it might be viewed as a "little victory" for the other dog or human. Dogs don't want their actions to be interpreted as "fleeing the scene," so any movement must be slow and deliberate, as if nothing had happened. This is why dogs will walk away from other dogs very slowly. Maybe, if they've been sitting down, they'll throw in a few stretches of the back legs or go to sniff something on the ground that all of a sudden seems very interesting.

**!**

## YOUR DOG CAN BE LIKE YOU

Studies have shown that neurotic owners end up with neurotic dogs, mostly because they are trained and disciplined inconsistently and end up in a state of conflict. Overaffectionate owners end up with dogs that display signs of dominance aggression toward them, because the dogs are allowed to get their way all the time.

# "Too intense, man."

Dogs often close their eyes to break up the intensity of a moment. Humans love to get up close and personal with their pets. This can all be a bit too much for their pets, who can't deal with the proximity and the physical contact as well as the eye contact in the moment. This is sometimes interpreted as a dog "really loving" the human touch, when in reality they are stuck with it and are just managing it the only way they know.

## "CHECK OUT THIS STICK."

Dogs such as pit bulls love carrying sticks around long after a fetching game is over. They also like to pick up sticks that are too large to be thrown and take them home. It's a prey substitute; they've killed this stick and they want to show it off.

# "I'm gonna take the cautious approach."

When dogs approach other dogs, they have to be wary of the consequences. In a public park, they will come across dogs of all shapes, sizes, and temperaments. A direct approach by one dog to another—running straight at them—can be very confrontational. Owners should be wary of other dogs who do this. For a dog, the best way to approach another is to sidle in, take a long, circular route, and join up with a new dog to see what it's like. Avoiding too much direct eye contact, sidling up, and even play-bowing will not offend a new dog and will open up a good opportunity for play.

# "I'm sca-a-a-a-red."

Though a dog's ears aren't quite as expressive as a cat's, they do show some fundamental emotions that are pretty easy to read. When a dog's ears are down, they are fearful or uncertain, and if interacting with another dog it is likely to be an act of submission easily read by the dog with greater status. The ears of a dog scurrying away with his tail between his legs will be the flattest they can get.

# "I'm interested."

When a dog's ears are pricked up, they are alert and interested, ready to hear more, ready to act on that sound at a moment's notice. Ears up and pointing forward are a sign of confidence.

# "I'm outta here!"

A frightened dog will have a combination of ears down and pulled back, wide eyes with large pupils, a lowered tail, a panting mouth, and he will be retreating or cowering. Fearful dogs will move to a position where they feel safest, a tucked-away corner where they can't be approached from behind.

## DEFENSIVE AGGRESSION

One of the reasons that a German shepherd is such a good guard dog is that it is genetically programmed to protect. It is a dog that is easily trained and learns quickly, so breeders built on this trait to develop better guard dogs.

# "I'm playing statues."

Dogs have four basic options open to them in a situation that could prove nasty. They can opt to flee, fight, perform an act of submission, or stay stock-still until the threat has passed.

Depending on the size and nature of the threat, they may use further "ignoring tactics" apart from their lack of motion, such as averting eye contact, turning the head away, walking off slowly, and pretending to find something interesting on the grass or sidewalk.

The staying-still option is a good tactic because it makes a dog's next movement unpredictable and keeps the other dog guessing. It also allows a dog further time to assess what the likely threat could be and if they should maybe change to an act of submission or an act of aggression—or simply escape!

# "Run for the hills, I am Cerberus!"

Dobermans, Rottweilers, and German shepherds make loving pets. They are also good guard dogs because they have little fear. It is often hard to tell what they are thinking in a family home because they show few of the signals of fear until they are tipped over the edge. Separating pups from the bitch too early, before they are fully socialized, will make it difficult for these dogs to get along with others.

Guard dogs are trained to view strangers as hostile; their levels of distrust are high. Approach carefully or opt for discretion and don't approach at all. They will display the classic aggression signs: erect body, direct unflinching stares, the desire to move forward directly at you (confusingly, they may wag their tail, too). If they are unleashed and barking, that's a good sign, since it shows a degree of fear even though they can attack you if they wish.

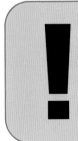

### DOGS FROM HELL

Cerberus was a monstrous dog of Greek mythology who guarded the gates to the underworld. He was the hound of Hades—a monstrous, three-headed dog with a snake for a tail and a serpentine mane. He made sure that the dead could not leave Hades and the living could not enter. His sister was Chimera and his brother was Orthrus.

# "This is a ball, right?"

In the relationship between dogs and humans, it is the dog that does most of the learning. In early puppyhood he will learn about interacting with others in the litter, in later puppy life he will start interacting with humans. The big shock for puppies is that humans greet them differently (no sniffing) and will do all sorts of bewildering things and expect them to react the right way.

# "Did I say you could pat me?"

The familiar greeting for a human to a dog involves a couple of things that wary dogs are not too fond of. First, a lot of direct eye contact; secondly, the hand thrust out near their heads to pat or stroke them. Most dogs will have learned to accept that this is the human way and will start to get familiar with it in puppyhood, when their cuteness factor is high. However, keeping your hands to yourself will generally make dogs less fearful.

Dogs would be happier with a good mutual sniff before taking the acquaintance further. They don't realize that human noses are not really up to the task.

## EARNING THEIR RESPECT

One of the important aspects of punishing a dog for bad behavior is to be consistent. Sometimes allowing it to get away with actions and then sometimes punishing it sends out very confusing signals. Similarly, using your dog's name for both praise and punishment is also confusing. That's why it's better to stick to the "good dog, bad dog" routine.

# "Two more minutes and that's enough."

Dogs that have grown up with a kind, loving family will be trained to accept the hands of many—patting them, stroking them, pulling them, holding them, and sometimes even grooming them. Dogs that have suffered from poor socialization as pups or have been treated badly by negligent, hurtful owners will find human contact very difficult to take. So not all dogs will be the same and a pet that is obtained from a rescue shelter may well have issues with human contact. The dog seen here is not comfortable with so much close contact but has learned to accept it as part of being the lowest-status member of the pack.

## THE GOLDEN RULES OF BEING THE BOSS

There are some golden rules about making sure it is you, the owner, who is in control of the household:

- Establish who's the boss when dogs are puppies.
- Train them as soon as you can.
- Deny them access to areas to show who's the boss.
- Control mealtimes; don't feed on demand.
- Don't let them win challenges, like a tug-of-war.
- On walks, don't let them stop at every fire hydrant.

# "Careful where you touch."

Even with a well-socialized dog that is used to being mauled by exuberant toddlers, there are areas where it would prefer not to be touched. Dogs are used to being touched along their backs and on their chests and heads, but they prefer not to be touched on their belly or between their hind legs. They can react by biting, though this pup has turned the session into a play-wrestle, with the softest of soft bites.

## PUNISH DOGS IMMEDIATELY

To discipline a dog successfully, the punishment must be administered immediately after the bad behavior has taken place. Owners have, literally, a matter of seconds to do it. Otherwise the dog becomes unsure about what it is being punished for. Even more effective is to preempt the behavior, to guess what it is about to do next—such as jumping up at a new guest—and disciplining it just as the behavior commences. This gives the strongest learning link of all.

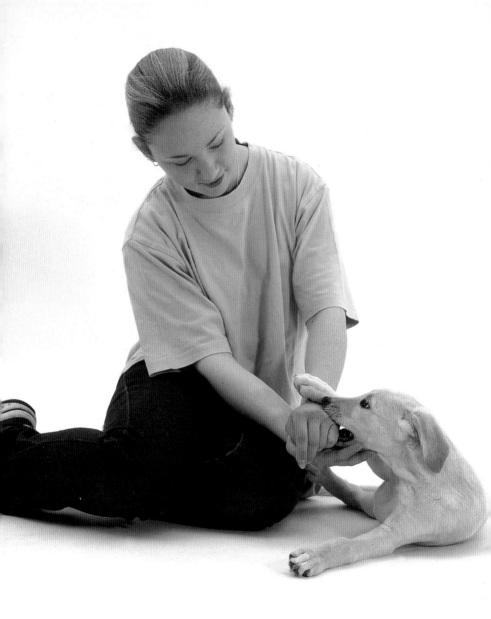

# "Don't mess with my head."

If a dog is going to bite someone, it is usually on the hand. Dogs don't really understand the need for all this human pawing of them, but they will go along with it. They use their paws to lock a bone in position, to nudge a friend into a chase or a play-fight, for mounting, and, of course, for running and standing. Humans use their hands for everything, including patting a dog's head, which dogs find neither soothing nor reassuring. All the finely tuned intelligence-gathering equipment is located in one area of the dog—ears, eyes, nose, and mouth—so a stranger who tries rough and insensitive contact around the head must do so with care. If a dog has suffered from harsh treatment to that area in the past, it could snap out at the stranger's hand. Behind the ears and along the jawbone are the places where a dog likes being stroked the best, but this should be done only once you have established a rapport with a dog.

# "Yes, that's good— very, very good."

There are places on a dog's body that itch like mad and cannot be reached unless an obliging human offers a helping hand. Most breeds love being scratched on their chests, around their collars, and behind their ears. With practice, owners soon find out where the "scratching joy" spots are and how much scratching is enough. Dogs will help by lifting paws, leaning into scratches to make the scratching pressure greater, or rotating their heads obligingly. This husky is getting a last-minute dose of human contact before beginning the grueling Iditarod Trail Sled Dog Race.

## THE BRAVEST HUSKY

Siberian huskies love cold weather, but sometimes that love is pushed to the limit. In the winter of 1925 they gained recognition when a diphtheria epidemic struck in Nome, Alaska. With the railroad blocked, dogsleds traveled over 650 miles through blizzards and subzero temperatures to get the antibiotics through. This act is commemorated by a statue of Balto, the lead dog of the team.

# "I could sit here a-a-a-a-a-ll day."

Scratching a dog's chest or behind its ears is actually an imitation of the contact a dog gets during courtship. Male dogs appreciate being rubbed on their chests because that is the area that is rubbed when a dog mounts a bitch. Due to the infrequency of real-life mating situations for male dogs, the stroking by an owner is about all they can look forward to. Likewise, the scratching or gentle massaging of a dog's ears are the closest substitutes to certain courtship rituals that dogs will be able to enjoy.

## DEWCLAWS

**!**

The small "toes" that dogs possess on the side of the foot are known as dewclaws. These are vestiges from a time when dogs were a climbing and running animal. In the past 10,000 years, the climbing part of their makeup has shrunk to nothing and so, too, has the dewclaw. Though they're usually found on the front legs of dogs, some breeds will have them on their hind legs. Many dog breeders cut them off just after the pups are born, as they think of them as unsightly. However, owners of Great Pyrenees recognize dewclaws as being part of the dog's genealogy and retain them.

# "You sure about that?"

Dogs frequently change the angle of their heads when they are puzzled or confused about something. The tilt of the head changes the position of the dog's ears relative to the source of the sound, helping the dog zero in on the source more accurately.

## TOP 20 MALE DOG NAMES

| | |
|---|---|
| 1. Max | 11. Charlie |
| 2. Jake | 12. Jack |
| 3. Buddy | 13. Harley |
| 4. Bailey | 14. Toby |
| 5. Sam | 15. Rusty |
| 6. Rocky | 16. Murphy |
| 7. Buster | 17. Shelby |
| 8. Casey | 18. Sparky |
| 9. Cody | 19. Barney |
| 10. Duke | 20. Winston |

# "Hey, this should do the trick!"

There's a film clip that is constantly replayed on TV shows about funny animals, in which a shepherd is talking about his dogs. While he is being interviewed, behind him one of his Border collies performs the perfect scooting act. The dog is sitting on a bank of grass and then toboggans down on his rump, with his front paws paddling away to keep him balanced. It looks like the dog is clowning around for the camera, but this is actually a hygiene issue. Dogs that "scoot" are often trying to free up their anal glands, which add the dog's own personal smell to its feces. If these glands are blocked and not giving out the right smell, the dog will lose some of its identity. When it meets other dogs, they won't get a true sense of who this dog is if they can't get the full smell. Scooting helps dogs regain their identities.

## TOP 20 FEMALE DOG NAMES

| | | | |
|---|---|---|---|
| 1. Maggie | 6. Daisy | 11. Dakota | 16. Missy |
| 2. Molly | 7. Ginger | 12. Katie | 17. Sophie |
| 3. Lady | 8. Abby | 13. Annie | 18. Bo |
| 4. Sadie | 9. Sasha | 14. Chelsea | 19. Coco |
| 5. Lucy | 10. Sandy | 15. Princess | 20. Tasha |

# "I'm in stink heaven!"

Much to their owners' dismay, many dogs like to roll in unmentionable filth. Some dogs seem to find perverse pleasure in locating the stinkiest animal droppings around and then repeatedly rolling in them, as though they're in the grips of some ecstatic passion. There are many theories as to why a dog does this, but one of the most convincing is that, because it is an animal that puts such a great importance on sniffing its peers' anal glands, having two strong, dunglike scents on its body is an added attraction. Getting ahold of that extra smell to add to its fur is too much to resist. Think of it as layering perfume—the base scent is the dog's own odor and it suddenly seizes on the chance to add a free "tester" on top.

## ! THE DOG STAR

Sirius, the Dog Star, is the brightest star in the nighttime sky, with a visual apparent magnitude of -1.46, and is located in the constellation Canis Major. Sirius is the star that represents the dog's eye. Ancient Egyptians called it the Dog Star after the god Osiris, whose head resembled that of a dog's.

# "I don't know what came over me."

As any owner will tell you, dogs may be dumb animals, but they're not stupid. They can be trained to do all kinds of sophisticated tasks. One dog is in the *Guinness Book of World Records* for performing 469 different tricks. And so, if a dog in a moment of excitement jumps up to look through a window and accidentally breaks an ornament, and they have experience of the reaction that this brings, then they can show guilt when the owner returns. The more intelligent the animal, the more likely they are to show guilt in the form of submissive body language—head and eyes lowered, stooped posture, and tail between legs. Some dogs will appear to be guilty because they can tell very quickly that their owner is angry.

## BAD DOG, NO DINNER . . . BUT A LOT OF DESSERT

At a New Year's Eve party the author attended, one of the guests insisted on bringing her Border collie inside because he was too cold outside in the car. The party went very well until it came to dessert, served just before midnight. A huge trifle had been left on a low shelf in the kitchen. When the hostess came to retrieve it, she saw the guiltiest-looking Border collie in the world with a nose covered in cream and hundreds of sprinkles.

# 98

# "You want a piece of me, big boy?"

Though behavior is universal among dogs (and wolves), there are various temperamental breeds that will not respond no matter how diligently you apply the lessons learned in this book. The Chihuahua is a particularly spiky dog that cannot abide other breeds in its pack or living with small children. It will be happy to reside with a member of its own breed or young adults, but no one else. It is also extremely combative when it is out on the street, with very little size or muscle to back it up. Which is why it's such a great thing to be able to tuck one of these creatures away in a coat pocket!

## ! SET YOUR WATCH BY THEM

Dogs have very good body clocks and can even time things, such as their owner's alarm going off each morning, to within sixty seconds over a twenty-four-hour period.

# "That's the whole point."

Pointers are a type of gundog that have been bred to detect the scent of prey and point toward it. Although the line of the dog's eyes may reveal the distance, all it can do is point in the direction of the scent. The accompanying humans then use their guns when the game bird or rabbit emerges from cover. Other breeds of dogs also retain a small ability to point in the direction of prey—it's another inherited wolf trait. When members of the wolf pack smell their prey, they point in the direction of the scent to communicate to others who have not picked it up yet. Thus the message is silently and easily communicated within the pack. This dog has spotted a squirrel in the undergrowth and, although the angle of its body isn't quite right, it's still typical pointing behavior.

## A BETTER WOLF

Humans have been able to breed "a better wolf" than nature by accentuating all the basic wolf characteristics. Bloodhounds are better at following scent, greyhounds are much faster, huskies have greater endurance, and Rottweilers are better at attacking. The most popular breed of dog is the closest in resemblance to a wolf—the German shepherd.

# "I'm fine now, but don't try to leave."

Weimaraners are latecomers to the world of pet dogs. They were bred as elegant gundogs, but were hardly known outside of Germany, where they were highly prized, until the 1930s and 1940s when the Weimaraner Club of America was formed. The babying tendency of owners through its breeding history has produced a dog that needs to be near humans and hates being put into kennels. The Weimaraner can suffer badly from separation anxiety and may start to panic if separated from its owner. It can also resort to aggression if the owner attempts to leave by trying to nip the owner's ankles and may engage in destructive behavior when the owner is gone, even going as far as self-mutilation. As these dogs grow older, the anxiety becomes less pronounced.

## ! THE "GRAY GHOST"

Weimaraners are known as "gray ghosts" for the stealthy way they hunt game in the field. President Dwight D. Eisenhower owned a Weimaraner named Heidi.

# Index

# Acknowledgments

The publishers would like to thank Warren Photographic for supplying the bulk of images for the book.
© Warren Photographic/Jane Burton: Pages 9, 10, 14, 17, 19, 20, 22, 25, 26, 29, 30, 31, 32, 35, 36, 38, 43, 44, 47, 51, 59, 61, 63, 66, 70, 73, 76, 79, 80, 83, 87, 91, 92, 95, 97, 98, 106, 113, 115, 116, 119, 120, 123, 127, 129, 130, 134, 136, 139, 147, 148, 152, 155, 157, 158, 161, 162, 165, 166, 170, 171, 172, 175, 176, 178, 181, 182, 185, 186, 191, 192, 196, 199, 200, 203, and 205.

© Warren Photographic: Page 7.
© Warren Photographic/Kim Taylor: Pages 52, 55, 56, 64, 69, 75, 84, 88, 101, 102, 109, 110, 124, 133, 140, 144, 151, 168, and 195.
© CORBIS: Cover image; pages 12, 40, 48, 105, 143, and 189.